KU
PRESS

RiPPLE 2022

A KINGSTON UNIVERSITY STUDENT ANTHOLOGY

18TH EDITION

RIPPLE 2022

A KINGSTON UNIVERSITY STUDENT ANTHOLOGY

THE 2022 RIPPLE TEAM

KINGSTON UNIVERSITY PRESS

First published in 2022 by Kingston University Press.

ISBN 978-1-909362-58-1

Typeset in Bebas Neue, FreightTextPro, Permanent Marker

Photographs/artwork © Felicia Beck, Zoe Bott, Isha Jan, Gabriel Liu, Liberty Rainbird-Jervis, Blu Selby, Marisa Spence, Wei Xinwei

Editorial and Design by Kingston University MA Publishing Students

KINGSTON UNIVERSITY PRESS
Kingston University
Penrhyn Road
Kingston-upon-Thames
KT1 2EE

www.kingstonripple.wordpress.com
Instagram account: @ripple_kingston

2022
RiPPLE TEAM

MANAGING EDITOR
Sophie Boddington

DEPUTY EDITORS
Amanda Carungi
Maria Nae

SENIOR COPY EDITORS
Kayleigh Kenworthy
Olivia Pucella

PRODUCTION MANAGER
Maya Conway

ART DIRECTOR
Molly Kellond

EBOOK DESIGNER
Bex Eastwell

JUDGING TEAM
Aríel Bertelsen
Ashmi Bhatt
Rachel Cotton
Bethany Crow
Georgina Dent
Kelsey Gould
Ida Langeland Hagen
Theodora Neacsu
Sianez Osman
Vanshika Parmar
Aneri Shah
Marisa Spence
Krishna Sunilkumar
Dessie Tsvetkova

EDITORIAL TEAM
Aríel Bertelsen
Rachel Cotton
Bethany Crow
Georgina Dent
Hanyun Hu
Ida Langeland Hagen
Sianez Osman
Vanshika Parmar
Krishna Sunilkumar
Dessie Tsvetkova

MARKETING TEAM
Annalisa Berdin
Senait Mekonnen
Marisa Spence
Courtney Thompson

2022
CONTENTS

2022
CONTENTS

ACKNOWLEDGEMENTS

Though we can't claim to have had the most challenging year to be a student (or anyone, really!), throughout 2021-2022, we've faced of rapid succession of changes – to public health, to how we can work, and how we interact socially. Yet one of the few true constants has been the tireless work put into RiPPLE. Presented with a huge number of submissions and our own strict deadlines, I have been fortunate enough to be surrounded by a team of tirelessly passionate and hardworking people, from our panel of student judges to our marketing team, editors and talented designers. It's often said that it takes a village to raise a child; it certainly takes no fewer to produce an anthology.

To single out the contributions made by every invaluable team member would most likely fill a separate book. But I would like to mention the singularly essential support of my Deputy Editors, Amanda Carungi and Maria Nae. From the excitement of hosting podcast episodes to the fine detail of editorial work, these two ladies have supported the creation of RiPPLE 2022 from the very beginning, and I could not be more grateful for their efforts. I am also indebted to the expertise of Emma Tait, the Course Leader for MA Publishing, whose practical knowledge and wisdom have been crucial to the continued success of this project.

Of course, none of this would even be possible without the skill and originality of the writers, poets and visual artists who submit to their work to us. Every year RiPPLE pushes boundaries with the scope of its work: this year is no different, with a truly astounding range of genres, mediums and subjects, from thoughtful explorations of the lingering effects of the pandemic, to breath-taking short stories of fantasy and fiction. On behalf of everyone at RiPPLE, we cannot wait to see what this incredible group of creatives produce in the future.

Finally, to you, dear reader. Thank you for picking up this year's RiPPLE and being the audience this work deserves.

SOPHIE BODDINGTON
Managing Editor, RiPPLE 2022

NO.1

A BAD ROMANTICISM

JASMINE HIGGINS

when living in london still felt new
my most favourite thing
was being sad on the tube

strangers passed right through me
like ghosts, or thoughts
little sparks of madness
i'd think 'how funny, they don't have a clue
that they're in my story'
main character complex
but who was it hurting?
except, well, probably me
i'd walk like i was everyone's unknown dream
floating up escalators
up, up, all the way
towards nothing, towards infinity

and none of that really matters now
i'm older, duller, wiser
and the city is nothing new
but sometimes i miss
being sad on the tube

NO.2
A FAIR TRADE

COURTNEY THOMPSON

It had been raining for two days straight and there was a thin layer of water over the patio, like a tide pool slowly filling as the waves came crashing in. An ecosystem had even begun to thrive there – little spotted frogs leapt through the water and snails perched themselves on the edges of the steps where the rainwater pooled. A few bright orange newts appeared now and then, finding hiding spots in patches of grass and fallen leaves.

Wynona noticed none of this as she stepped into the garden, her heavy rain boots cutting through the water and kicking up large droplets. She pulled the cords of her raincoat to tighten the hood. Bits of her hair hung loose, quickly getting damp from the downpour. She let them be and trudged forward, her dark shape moving across the gloomy sky.

Surveying the yard, Wynona looked past its new inhabitants, instead searching for a pop of red against all the greys and greens. She splashed her way over to the two-story shed, finding nothing of use. The rake had fallen over and was lying in the water, probably beginning to rust. She didn't bother to pick it back up. The forgotten dog toy wedged in between the shed and the fence she left, too.

She felt water seeping into her shoes where the rubber soles had torn, and she considered going back inside, but the wailing started back up again, piercing through the ornate glass panels of the garden door. She sighed and continued walking along the perimeter of the fence, her socks beginning to squelch inside her boots.

Beneath the water, there was only the well-trimmed grass. Even the frogs had vanished, scurrying out of the way of Wynona's thundering steps. When she had made her way throughout the entirety of the garden, the ends of her hair sufficiently dampened and her socks soaked through, she sighed and returned to the door. Walking up the short flight of stairs, she spotted a bit of red through the slots between them. She took a step back and crouched to examine it – the little red race car lay floating in a deep puddle under the steps. She squeezed her hand through the gap and pulled it out, nearly kissing the little plastic car despite the muck that coated it. She held it under the rainfall for a moment to rinse it off and went inside, carrying it like it was made of gold.

The crying was overwhelming when she opened the door. She wiped her shoes once on the flowery mat and followed the sound, leaving behind muddy footprints and a trail of water that dripped from her coat and shoes. The little boy was slumped in the living room, a pile of toys and games littering the floor nearby, but his hands empty. Big tears fell down his chubby face, the kind that only children seem to produce, almost cartoonishly plopping down onto the sheepskin rug.

'Hey,' Wynona said, crouching down beside him. 'I found your car.'

He looked up, his face all red and snotty. The crying instantly ceased.

'My race car!' He reached for it, but Wynona pulled her hand back and held the car high in the air.

'First you have to tell me where Mommy keeps her jewellery, okay? A deal's a deal.'

The boy looked up at the race car with wide eyes. 'She has a box in her room, way up high in the closet. She puts sparkly things in it.'

Wynona smiled and handed him the toy car. 'Thanks kid.'

He grabbed the race car and began sliding it across the floor, making vroom noises to mimic an engine. Wynona turned away, her socks still squelching, and picked up the black backpack she'd left near the back door. The little garden dwellers re-emerged to enjoy the rain as she made her way to the parents' bedroom.

NO.3

A HALLOWTIDE MIRACLE

DANIELLE KNIGHT

Once, there was a royal orchard.

The land gathered around was bitter and cruel, but the orchard! 'Twas the Queen's pride. From early spring to late autumn, every tree was heavy with ripe, juicy apple-fruit, for which our Queen had a great lust.

Every tree but the Barren Tree.

When the royal fruit-pickers came to fill their baskets, the Barren Tree's branches were as empty as her sisters' were dense. However, she thought herself content.

Her sister-trees agreed to warn her: 'If you don't bear fruit, what reason has the Queen to keep you? Soon, the woodcutter will come a-chopping.'

The Barren Tree shed sap-tears as the fruit-pickers worked their way round her. How stupid she'd been! To think she'd go on living without bearing fruit!

And so, she prayed. For years and years, she prayed for fruit of her own. But the God-Tree did not answer. Eventually, her cries reached the God-Spider. He descended from the heavens on a silver thread, ripening apples in His presence till their branches bowed.

'My lady,' said He, 'why do you cry. . . and so shrilly?'

'The Queen shall have me chopped if I don't bear fruit!'

The God-Spider laughed. 'No need to cry! This is easily righted.'

Quick as a thought, He buried an egg in her bark, climbed His silver thread, and went about His business.

Before long, the egg in her trunk had grown fat. 'Twas not the kind of fruit-bearing she'd had in mind, but no doubt this miraculous event would thrill the Queen more than any apple pie. Her sisters' apples turned sour – so envious were they! – and she couldn't have been happier.

But alas! All was not well in the orchard. The royal fruit-pickers were so afeared of the thing that grew like a belly from her mangled trunk that none would brave the picking. The bounty of sweet-fleshed fruit began to rot, and not one graced the Queen's table.

She promised royal riches to aspiring heroes, but none came to solve the issue. Who'd risk their soul for riches? The demon tree was proof that the orchard was cursed.

So said all but Helenor.

When news of riches reached her ears, she dropped her chickens and took up her axe. There was no husband to stop her from striding into the orchard at dusk, pulping overripe apples under her boot.

The mother-to-be heard the leaves whispering: 'Too little, too late to thrill the Queen! She has decided to chop you anyway; her woodcutter comes with axe in hand!'

O, woe! To be struck down while heavy with spider! It's true, the tree feared for herself, though maternity had changed her raison d'être. Now, her thoughts turned to the legacy she'd leave behind.

'I would gladly sacrifice my own life,' she cried, 'if it meant my spiderlings might live!'

Helenor reached the tree and saw the fruit-pickers' fear at once.

O, horrors! This tree!

What twitching villainy waited inside the gelatinous bulge? Evil-smelling, it was dripping with olive-coloured slime that charmed flies.

When the tender God-Spider dragged His majestic bulk from the heavens, Helenor's blood turned colder still. What a monster! Velvet-black, huge as a horse – a most repulsive creature!

'Strike this tree,' said He, 'and you strike the spiderlings I've fathered on her.'

'Indeed,' said Helenor, little dreaming she spoke to a god. She struck the tree's swollen trunk with her axe, killing the unborn spiderlings with one blow.

Even the sister-trees cringed. How heartless, this butcher-woman!

Helenor fled in want of a good, stiff brandy. What nightmares she could look forward to, now that she'd seen the God-Spider and His rancid cradle. What shivers she'd gift her sisters' brats when she tucked them into bed.

The tree lived to mourn her spiderlings, wailing louder than any banshee.

'Weep not, my lady,' the God-Spider said. 'We'll try again.'

When Helenor made it back, she delivered the happy news that made her a hero. Her name was thusly set in song: Helenor, the Spider-Hater.

The Queen got her apples and Helenor, her riches. She was done cooping chickens and would never again sell eggs. She bought a very fine manor, and plenty of help to keep it fine.

Helenor remained a spinster. But a spinster in silks!

Still, her sisters worried for her. 'If you don't marry soon, you'll lose your chance.'

Helenor gave a great belly laugh. With riches already in her account, what want for marriage could there be?

Her sisters knew that if she didn't listen, she'd certainly die alone. Even with riches, husbands were impossible to find.

Almost a year had passed before the Queen called on Helenor anew. That blighted tree – fat with spider-spawn again!

Helenor didn't complain. She'd a taste for delicious living now, and delicious living didn't come cheap. Manors, help, silks, it all cost money. But she needn't resort to marriage;

another heroic deed, and the Queen would lavish more coin upon her.

Her orchard visit set the leaves a-whispering. When word reached the Barren Tree, she cried.

The God-Spider descended, and implored Helenor: 'Compassion, good lady! 'Tis this tree's great wish to bear fruit – you'd deny her that?'

'Indeed,' said Helenor, killing the unborn spiderlings with one blow. She'd no thoughts of chopping down the money tree. With any luck, it'd grow fat again, and more often!

She bolted, screaming with laughter.

The tree's wailing reached a fever pitch: 'I cannot bear this heartbreak again! Besides, my body is at its limit!'

The God-Spider winced and left. This would not do! He had to find some other way to move this so-called hero, Helenor.

He sent little spider-spies to Helenor's very fine manor. They filled the corners and crevices and watched. They saw Helenor, and her help, and nobody else in her gloomy abode. No hale and hearty husband, and no sweet babes. The God-Spider recognized her problem at once: loneliness, the most desperate struggle of all.

The God-Spider returned to the Barren Tree.

'Fear not, sweet lady,' said He, giving her another egg to cradle. 'I know the object that will sweeten this murderess to your purpose.'

He had a plan to please both parties.

* * *

Helenor next spoke with the Queen near Hallowtide. Turnip lanterns sat like shrunken heads on steps all o'er the queendom.

She had just celebrated her thirty-ninth name day. While she drank, her sisters' brats scurried round, snot-nosed. The fathers were farmers and fish-sellers and fence-menders without pots to piddle in. Helenor pitied her sisters, and her sisters pitied her.

Poor Helenor; she would die childless. They saw the marriage-shaped hole she tried to fill with brandy and spider-slaying. What a desperate, empty life!

Of course, Helenor's riches would soon be so great, she need not fear any demand for marriage. At the snap of her fingers, the help lifted her axe from its mount. She took to the orchard that night, grinning like a madwoman.

But a white fog wrapped the trees, so thick she could not see which path she took. Within minutes, Helenor was lost.

Hours of wandering later, she arrived at a cottage. It floated on the fog like a delusion – she knew there was no such building in the orchard – but exhaustion clouded her judgement. Besides, its windows glowed warm from the fire within, and a most delicious scent hung in the air. Sticking her axe in a stump, she mounted the porch steps.

She rapped her knuckles on the door – who opened it, but a hale and hearty woodcutter?

'You must be lost,' he said. 'Best come in till the fog clears. I've belly-stuffs aplenty.'

Helenor shuffled inside and saw he told no lies. No fish-bladder beer or dry folk-cakes for the woodcutter's table, O no! A spread fit for a queen lay before her: potato pancakes with jammed apples, cinnamon goats cheese with braised apples, offal dumpling stew with stewed apples...

And she, the only guest!

Had she not been so fatigued, she might have seen the metal trap round this phantasmic cheese, waiting to snap down on her neck.

As it was, her stomach gurgled with sudden, painful hunger beneath her silk coat. She seated herself at the table and, seeing the woodcutter use his hands to eat, spurned her cutlery.

She ate slowly... at first.

* * *

Faster and faster, she stuffed her cheeks, till her coat unbuttoned, her chin ran with sauce, and she knew that if another crumb touched her lips, she would pop, and yet. . .

Only once, she thought of stopping. When she caught the woodcutter's eye. There was something in that eye. Something premeditated and beastly. Her eyes were drawn to a silver pin on his coat. Damned if it didn't look exactly like a spider.

But raindrops the size of eggs thunk-thunk-thunked onto the roof. Even Helenor daren't brave that weather, so she went back to feasting.

When the rain eased, Helenor could not stand. She dozed off where she sat, face half-buried in a potato pancake-pillow, mouth a snoring O.

Gone was the fire-glow when Helenor awoke. Not even embers lingered in the ashes. Dark green mould stained the table, fungi blossomed from the walls and threads of silver glittered in moonlit corners.

The plates: cleared away. The fair woodcutter: nowhere to be thanked for his generosity. She'd not asked the fellow's name. Shameful, really.

Helenor scraped her chair back, glanced down, and choked a little.

She'd feasted so vigorously that her belly had swollen to the size of a brandy barrel! The skin was stretched tight and, try as she might, she couldn't force her coat buttons to their fastenings. What had possessed her to eat so much?

Bafflingly, she felt as hungry as if she had eaten nothing all night.

As she hoisted herself from the chair, the undigested meal twitched in her tummy most unpleasantly. Had her dinner been lively as she ate it? She waddled down the porch steps to retrieve her axe, and each one complained of her weight.

At least the fog had cleared. She slowly found her way to the Barren Tree, axe-blade dragging in the dirt behind her. No God-Spider came to stop her, but... where was the vile, gelatinous growth?

The trunk looked as though it'd been torn open by scavengers. 'Twas white like a melted wax candle, and Helenor tasted death in the air: dank rot, and something oily and metallic, like fresh offal.

No matter, the sun was rising. In Helenor's mind, the spiderlings were gone, and nobody needed to know she hadn't been the one to get rid of them. She would simply tell the Queen the demon tree was slain, collect her bounty and go on living deliciously.

Helenor toddled back to deliver her happy news, and the God-Spider watched from the heavens. How clever He was, and how generous, fixing both ladies' problems in one fell swoop!

What He carried off was nothing short of a Hallowtide miracle, for Helenor cradled the Barren Tree's legacy. Come the 'morrow, she'd deliver their spiderlings into the world, her once-empty manor crawling with sweet children. The God-Spider had no doubt they'd bring tremendous joy to their surrogate mother, along with the whole queendom.

Helenor's spider-hating days were long behind her.

NO.4

A LETTER TO MY INNER CHILD

RACHEL ESSEX

We were just a child
When those familiar faces wrapped their vines around us
And sliced our skin with their greedy touch.
They decided we were their favourite flower
And plucked us from the garden of childhood.
We were placed into mounds,
Left without water, without food, and without stability.
Nobody noticed the change in our petals,
The way they would rip apart at the slightest touch,
Or how their colour faded from a blossoming yellow
To a dull grey.
But even grey can be silver in the right lighting.
We began to re-root ourselves,
Learning new ways to bloom,
Until we were torn from the mound
And the flower that we used to be lay wilted in their
    calloused hands.

Rest child, I will wake you soon.
Maybe when the trees are barren, and the flowers no
    longer bloom.
Maybe when the sound of laughter has ceased to exist.
Or maybe when the last flame has dwindled and lays its head
    to rest,
Surrounded by the ashes of the people we once knew, and the
    people we never got to meet.

NO.5

ANOTHER GOSSIP

RAAJEEV AUCHAMBIT

Fast-Fast, I gossip about Mauritius with my mother-in-law:
'You know... You're staying in a stable country,'
And her hands immediately give a chapati,
In praise, of God, her mother-in-law's culinary skills.

Untroubled by kitchen politics,
They help each other, like one bag of tricks.
'Put more sugar,' she orders.
'No bittersweet division,' the other continues.

For we are Mothers-in-law under fair laws;
Made by this merry Motherland.

Fast-Fast, I gossip about Mauritius with my grandchildren:
'You know... You live in harmony here,'
And they quickly click a selfie with me inside;
Outside, with the prevailing tranquillity.

They post online,
And together, we like and share
Positive vibes
With our frenemies.

As a composed clique;
We remain the Grandchildren of this Grand Island.

Fast-Fast, I gossip about Mauritius with my husband:
'You know... Everyone says, I share the same relaxing voice as
    the country.'
He laughs badly, and pokes:
'What, again? No comparison with marvellous Mauritius!'

We fight for a while,
Them smile widely;
'Not disciples of Pran and Lalita Pawar,' blindly, we agree
    to follow:
Love.

Of a cuddling ease,
Coupled within a bubble of no trouble, families are content
    to stay here.

NO.6

ART EDUCATION

WEI XINWEI

BITTER

SKYE PRICE

Her world was dipped in fire
Soaked in molten lava
Every natural disaster
Surged one after the other

She held on to the anger
It was a gnawer and a biter
Claws out, gripped tighter
Vomit up the trauma

Words spat out in bile
Her insides settled stale
She did not light the match
But she nurtured the flames so well

NO.8

COMPLICATED INDIFFERENCE

HANNAH TAYLOR

There I was. Looking in the reflection. I could see myself behind Annie's figure, slanted slightly on top of her handbag. She stares anxiously in the mirror like that every day. Every day before she leaves for work. It's tiresome being her phone. She's around toxic people. She doesn't know it yet because she's oblivious, the sort of owner who over worries about herself; and she doesn't realize the mistake she's making. She needs to look further. She brings me into the office five days a week. It's not like I have legs to walk away. I am left on her desk. Abandoned to suffer the squeals of the high-pitched friends who long to get away and post their selfies on several social media platforms. Annie doesn't interact that way. She's much more of an in-the-moment person, someone who prefers the face-to-face conversation.

At last, Shirley arrives. She's late as always and uses the same inept excuse: she's simply too busy caring for her 148 cats to be on time. Then comes the powerful grand entrance of the decorative honey-coloured cake. She's usually a master of lying, yet today she can't seem to look anyone in the eye when she tells them she spent all night baking. The people can't see, the cake is in place of an apology, one she can't bring herself to give. The team overindulge in sycophantic enjoyment in something that is eaten and forgotten in just a few minutes. That's Shirley's work done for the day.

Meanwhile, Annie is psyching herself up for her next meeting in the spare office. She can't stand the place as much as I do. The boss strolls in, 'Everyone alright? You alright, Jeannie? Good.' That's his job. He asks a few questions and scurries back to his brain-numbing phone games behind his 'supreme', elevated desk. At this point, Annie comes back and shoves me into her bag. I can still hear the nonsensical, muffled sounds through the silk-lined material. Pete is on the verge of shouting as he converses with Dan over the weekend football results. Ping! Annie forgot to turn me on silent. A message from her brother, Carter. She takes me out and I'm free again. She scans over the message. Today I'm slower than usual, too many updates that need Annie's approval. It must be important. She's taking me over to the big window - the one where people think the skyscrapers are somewhat scenic. Annie never stands here; it normally gives her vertigo. She seems occupied, as if she is no longer in the office and is back at home. Back where she is carefree and most importantly, herself. The message is gone. It's been deleted.

Annie's office-day today was as mundane as any other. Except her expression. It was different, she was glowing this time. A little too happy for an office worker. Especially for someone who works with such ordinary people. I witness life through tiny circles. I see and hear every detail in Annie's life: who gossips about her when she's not there, and the women who show insecurity with a flick of the side-eye. Annie's got someone in her life that really cares about her, someone who she isn't quite ready to meet. Someone who isn't yet ready to share the world with her.

We're back at home now. Away from the crazy menagerie, which people call their everyday jobs. Annie is turning on her Wi-Fi. She has seventy-two new emails. For some reason I can't read them. The inbox page is blank. Her finger scrolls through the page and stops. She's staring almost as if she can hear me. Dazed into her own reflection. She panics and hits the Contacts list. The name isn't there, only the number.

I haven't memorized her contact numbers; I've never needed to. The only day I need to work, and I keep... glitching. The person picks up after a few rings. Annie is cutting out; every other word is mumbled. 'Ne... today... order... Amazon.' The room is getting hotter. Annie is wearing a sweater; she doesn't look hot. She's doing her victory dance; she only does this when something really good has come her way. She's moving me side to side. Normally she takes more care of her phone. Annie's had me for ages. I'm her best possession. She's fiddling with the volume button. Suddenly, the call is clearer. It's her brother's voice. He says, 'The order has gone through. It should be here tomorrow.' Annie replies, 'Thanks, I can't wait for a new one.' An email pops up. It reads: 'Carter has gifted you with a new...'. A big picture of the latest Samsung model fills the whole page. The battery icon flashes to 4%. Annie isn't rushing to find the plug.

CURVE

MORGAN BRATLI

I know from where you come
Down those sloping hills
The pines of earthen touch carry coloured prongs
Of sound and paper crumpling
Sleep, if you please
Then
Cup your soul and spool your prow
Did I live, if ever
When how or where
A regret leaked from my swollen craw
For the rhythm I never had
Rest, give it here
But do not leave, I wish to linger longer
If my choosing I will die
Amongst purblind strangers
Part the curtains
And eat the fruit when ripe
However rotten to chew
If on it, I choke
Does it mean you will too?

NO.10

DEAR PRE-COVID LOVER

JASMINE HIGGINS

we haven't talked since before everything
november streets, handholding
pedestrian crossing buttons
pressed with bare fingers, not through sleeves
back when you could learn a person
by watching their lips as they speak

now we look in strangers' eyes from a distance
wonder if their eyebrows were always so expressive
or if it's 2020's evolution
forcing connection with someone
who can't see who you are
every shy voice forced louder than ever

it's not all bad, really
i've been doing okay through all this
early mornings, new rituals
not that you really asked
i think we all quit asking,
how've you been?
when the default answer changed
from good, thanks to well, you know

we met before the masquerade
when every sea of strangers
became a sea of danger
every creature painted bad
by the tainted air around them

and in this new world
where the old is forgotten,
never to return
i'm not sure what to say to you
after all this
i'm not sure we know each other
anymore

NO.11

EQUIDISTANT

MARIA NAE

The vast pool swallowed Evie's frail body whole as she dived head-first into the cool water. She swam, her aching limbs struggling to keep up with her racing mind. 'I can do it,' she told herself over and over again. 'I can win the competition; I just need to practise.'

After five laps, she closed her eyes and allowed the water to quiet the voice in her head. She let her tired body slowly sink, the blue silky liquid welcoming her in a cold embrace. Inhale - the overpowering smell of chlorine. The intense quietude seemed to close in on her at a steady pace. Exhale. Short blonde hair surfaced around her pale face like a halo. The corners of her mouth turned upwards into a peaceful smile as a ray of warm sunlight penetrated the window above and caressed her freckled face. This was her place.

She floated there, still. 'Huh,' she thought. 'There is an equal distance between me and either side of the pool... I am equidistant.'

Opening her eyes, Evie realised she often felt like that. Equidistant. As if she was never fully anywhere, but always between things, places, people. She got out of the pool and wrapped herself in a towel.

'Come on, darling,' her mother said. 'We're meeting your aunt for tea and cake at Ole & Steen.'

Evie did not love her aunt. In fact, she barely tolerated the woman. She was loud and fake, and constantly gossiping about things like who her neighbour was dating now or that her co-worker got plastic surgery. Evie could not comprehend why anyone would pay so much attention to other people's lives, as if it changed their own. She wanted to stay home, make a cup of peppermint tea, cuddle up next to Volt, her beloved ginger cat, and read to her heart's content. That stillness, that peace of being alone – but not lonely – was all she wanted. Dressed, she walked outside with her mother.

It was a beautiful day. The sky was bright blue for a change and not a speck of cloud could be seen. There were people everywhere. Walking down St. James's street, hand in hand, some singing, some talking, but everyone seemed happy, energetic. Out of the corner of her eye, Evie spotted a group of young women in short dresses and heels, singing and holding cups with a dark yellow substance she assumed was apple juice. One of the women fell over and the others laughed, instead of helping their friend.

'How odd,' Evie thought. That feeling of not being completely in her own body returned. She was happy to be out and about in the sun, but half of her longed for that tranquillity. Maybe that's what the pandemic did to people. Maybe everyone felt like that. Deep inside her that familiar flickering candle turned into a spark that began to take form and grow into a flame. She wanted to live, not just be alive. Not anymore.

NO. 12

FIRST LOVE?

CLARA CHACON GAMARRA

First love
or delusion?

Pure?

WITHERED

Inside,
a little coffin

without
your colour
there is not
allusion
not even
an illusion

not desire
to wait
...or...
longing you

my single
decision
so simple
and plain
will be
to forget
...
you

NO.13

FORGET

WEI XINWEI

NO.14

HAMPTON WICK EARTHWORK: STEEL OBJECT DRAWING PLANS

CAMERON MOWAT

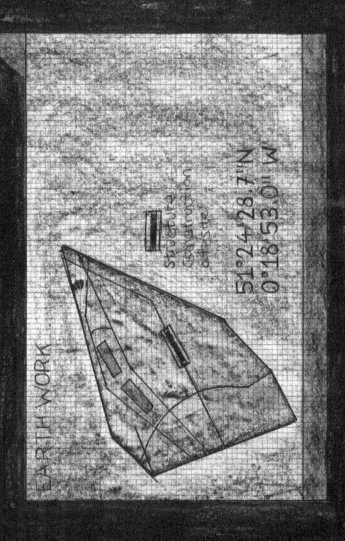

EARTH WORK

Structure
(Construction)
on site

51°24'28.7"N
0°18'53.0"W

NO.15

HAMPTON WICK EARTHWORK: ATMOSPHERE CONCEPT SKETCH & MATERIAL MODEL TEST

CAMERON MOWAT

NO. 16

HAMZA'S LOON

MICHAEL VOWLES

Out on the lake a pair of loons rounded the nearest island. They made their way across the lake side by side. Sometimes they dove beneath the water when they spotted a leech or a crayfish, but the couple always reassembled itself.

* * *

Aubree seemed a lot more relaxed now that they were finally here.

'Hey, you can't be nervous,' Bryan had teased her back in the car. 'They're your family. How'd you think I feel?'

'I'm not nervous,' she protested.

'Liar.'

The Bauer cabin was built into a hill that poked out of the forest, the various levels of the property connected by a series of wooden staircases that zig-zagged up and down the escarpment. So far only Aubree's brother and father were here. The meeting had gone well enough, Bryan thought. A little stiff maybe. But this whole weekend was destined to be awkward.

They went around to the side, where Bryan stopped to admire a little rock garden tucked against a corner of the house. On the neat bed of innumerable, smaller stones were arranged six large, uneven rocks with flat sides facing up. Each rock had been hand-painted with a different colour combo, and on each one a different name was written. The left two rocks (orange-blue and red-yellow) belonged to the two men he'd just met, Aubree's father Rick, and brother Cameron. The right two (blue-white and pink-purple) read Kelsey and Heidi, who he knew were Aubree's sister and mother respectively. Bryan focused on the middle two, however, which seemed closer together than the other rocks. The green and yellow one was Aubree's. The other, red and white, belonged to Hamza.

'Neat,' Bryan said, his eyes lingering on the red and white one.

'Oh yeah,' Aubree said, as though she hadn't noticed the stones yet. 'Yeah, we all picked out our stones from the bottom of the lake.'

'I like it.'

Aubree glanced at them for a second before drifting away. A rumble of tires on gravel emerged from the pines and she shrieked, running over to greet the car that was arriving. Bryan followed in her wake. As he rounded the corner of the cabin, Cameron came out of the door at the same time. Both men flinched. Bryan opened his mouth to make a joke out of it, but Cameron quickly averted his gaze and strode off toward the exterior staircase.

Three women had exited the car and were all hugging Aubree, who was squealing again. Heidi and Kelsey looked vaguely familiar to him, though Bryan was sure he had never actually met them. The third, a sturdy, dark-haired woman, he could infer was Lizzie – Cameron's steady girlfriend.

Bryan wondered if they all usually greeted each other this effusively, or if a special case was being made for Aubree. Then again, he reminded himself as he watched from the top of the steps, none of the Bauers had seen each other since the pandemic started. For some of them, it might even have been as far back as the funeral. When he went down to make his introductions, the usual two-metre Corona etiquette resumed – for which he was grateful. He had already shaken Rick's hand out of habit. Or maybe to show some kind of primitive deference. All three of the women seemed nice.

'I remember you,' Kelsey said. 'Your mom worked in the

school cafeteria.'

'She's still there.'

They decided to go out on the pontoon boat. Aubree told her father she was eager to give Bryan a tour of the whole lake. Rick headed down the staircase that led to the dock, while Cameron, Heidi, Kelsey, and Lizzie carried the grocery haul from the Mennonite store up the one that led to the cabin. Aubree and Bryan stayed on the middle level.

'Are you always this extra with your family?' Bryan asked as she slid her arms around his neck.

'What do you mean?' Aubree said, pouting at him.

'Nothing, I was just teasing.'

'Good. I'm glad you're here...'

Aubree leaned up and they kissed. The two of them held each other for a few moments before Aubree announced she was going to see if her dad needed any help with the boat. Bryan felt a prickle of sweat on the back of his neck. Turning around, he looked up at the deck just in time to see Cameron shuffle away.

* * *

As the day went on, Bryan became aware of a recurring pattern in the group conversations. Everyone – except for Cameron, who gave him a wide berth – was polite toward him, but none of them talked to him for as long as they could help it. Questions came with little-to-no eye contact, and there were never any follow-ups when he answered. With each other, the Bauers talked heartily, but never about anything that Bryan felt like he could contribute to. They would rise in tempo and then suddenly drop, as though they had just remembered he was there. It was a cycle of organic excitement, followed by lulls of self-consciousness. At first Aubree made several attempts to include him, but by the afternoon, even she was barely talking to him.

With the others, however, she spoke breathlessly. Bryan thought he noticed everyone's eyes linger on Aubree long after she finished talking, which made him wonder if she had always been this hyperactive. Cameron paid particular attention to her, as though she were a modern art piece he couldn't quite figure out.

That evening Rick put together a fish fry while the rest of them drank Spotted Cow and played card games on the deck. Bryan, who had gone back inside to change out of his swim shorts, hesitated before re-joining them. So far, he hadn't spent much time in the cabin itself. It was an eclectic place, in which no amount of space seemed unoccupied. Of the many things that vied for his attention, Bryan was drawn most of all to a series of paintings along the walls. A walleye, a muskie, an eagle. Tamarack swamps and old growth forests. A side view of a loon, as though drawn for a premodern field guide. Bryan stared into the lidless, blood-red eye and felt something like nausea. Yet, for whatever reason, he couldn't look away.

A toilet flushed nearby. Seconds later, Heidi emerged from a door down the hall. When she looked up, she seemed startled to find Bryan lingering there.

'I'm sorry, were you waiting to use the restroom?'

She didn't look much like Aubree, Bryan thought.

'No, no. I was just admiring these paintings here. Who's the artist?'

Heidi blinked, turning to look at the wall. There was an audible intake of breath when she did. She started nodding, gazing at the various scenes of rural Wisconsin and its fauna.

'Yes, they are nice,' she whispered, continuing to nod as she inspected each one. 'These are all Hamza's work.'

'Really?' Bryan exclaimed. 'They're amazing.'

Heidi smiled at that, as though it were her own son Bryan was complimenting. It felt like the first genuine smile he had gotten out of her since they met.

'Yes, they really are.'

'Are these all scenes from this lake?'

'Yes. Hamza really loved it up here.'

'I can tell.'

There was a pause. Heidi shifted her weight onto her other foot.

'Did… you know him?'

'No,' Bryan said. 'No, I never knew him.'

Heidi nodded once again, slower this time. She glanced back at the loon in front of them, before clearing her throat.

'Excuse me,' she said, and headed for the deck. Bryan stayed with the paintings a while longer. Outside he could hear Aubree laughing hysterically at something. Rather than going out to join them, he went into the bedroom where he and Aubree had left their bags. There were only two bedrooms in the cabin, but it seemed like it had already been assumed that he and Aubree would take one. Naturally, Rick and Heidi would take the other. That left Cameron and Lizzie the fold-out mattress and Kelsey, the couch. He recalled Aubree saying something along the lines that this had always been unofficially hers when he'd asked about arrangements.

He realized then that it was probably because she and Hamza had used it so often over the past ten years. His eyes fell on the bed. Bryan thought about all the times Hamza must have woken up in these sheets with Aubree in his arms, the sunlight on his face.

* * *

Bryan heard the door to the deck slide open, then close again. An aggressive burp reverberated around the cabin, and he followed the sound into the main room, where he found Aubree in a fit of giggles.

'Oh shit,' Bryan said. 'How many beers did you drink?'

Aubree stumbled toward him, still trying to contain her laughter.

'Why are you hiding in here? Hm? I think that's the real question.'

'I'm not, I was just admiring these paintings. Your mom told me that Hamza made them.'

'Oh, those…' Aubree said, not even glancing at them. 'Yeah… he was really talented.'

'I don't have any talent.'

'Me neither,' Aubree said.

'Hey, you're supposed to say: everyone has a talent.'

'Not like Hamza did.'

'Clearly.'

There was a long silence between them. Aubree frowned.

'Is something wrong?'

'No. Are you okay?'

'I'm fine,' Aubree said. Another long silence. Neither of them looked at each other. Bryan focused back on the red eye of Hamza's loon. Among the growing shadows, it looked menacing. Aubree stepped closer, swaying ever so slightly, until her nose touched his chin. 'Do you wanna... you know...' she purred into his ear.

'Jesus!' Bryan hissed, checking over his shoulder that no one else was in the cabin. 'Has your mind touched the void?'

'Come on...' Aubree said. 'I want you.'

'Aubs, your family is right there.'

'I don't care. Come on, let's go back to the room...'

'No way,' Bryan said, stepping out of reach. 'What's wrong with you?'

Aubree's face changed in an instant. At first, he was worried she was going to cry. Instead, she remained very still.

'What's wrong with me?' she said, raising her voice.

Bryan opened his mouth to speak just as Cameron came in the side door.

'That's enough beer for tonight. You need to drink some water.'

'Hey,' Cameron snapped. 'Don't tell her what to do man.'

Bryan winced. He knew that Cameron Bauer had been waiting over fifteen years for this. Seeing him standing there in the open doorway, nostrils flaring, cheeks flushed, Bryan remembered:

'Think fast, asshole!' The pigskin launched straight for Cameron's unsuspecting face. At the last second, he looked up. And out came the tooth.

Everyone had exploded in laughter. And worse, Cameron would be teased for the gap in his teeth for a whole year.

'It's okay, Cam,' Aubree assured him. Cameron remained in the doorway, the fist that held the handle shaking. 'Really. I'm so shit-faced.'

Cameron continued to glare at Bryan for a few more seconds before turning on his heel and disappearing down the exterior staircase. Bryan sighed.

'I should talk to him.'

'You should,' Aubree agreed. She staggered, balancing herself on a brick column in the centre of the living room. Then she said, 'I came in to tell you we're getting ready to release Hamza's balloons.'

'Do you need me?' Bryan asked. Aubree didn't answer him. 'Maybe it would be better if I sat it out. Let you be with your family.'

'Right.'

* * *

Bryan found Cameron sitting on the dock. Back up on the deck, the Bauers prepared the balloons. They were all bright colours. Heidi was insistent that, if anything, it was a celebration. Hamza would have been thirty-two that day.

The sky was grey going into black. The trees now seemed to join together in a singular dark print against the pale evening. The sun was gone, but its light lingered on the water's surface.

On the lake, the loon now made a lonesome silhouette. Uncoupled, it simply bobbed in the water, not knowing whether to swim or to fly.

NO.17

Hazy eyes

LISA MARIE SNEIJDER

In the wonder of a summer daze
Caught in a boastful stare of yesterday's eyes
Every sense trembles

I shiver

A look spoiled for pleasure
Masked in a twirl floating on its drum
Missing the syllables to express
The daunting assertiveness
Steered by the need to caress
While only bouncing shadows fill the air

I succumb

To keep turning and turning
Until the foggy shapes are no more
The eyes have wandered onto future prospects
Far beyond the hazy hour
Simply a stolen touch
Ingrained in that second without time
Back into those sultry lights

I stay

I CAN

SKYE PRICE

My nervous system is an explosion of lightning bolts
Playing a life-or-death game of Chinese whispers
At 11 million bits per second.

And in that second, 25 million new cells
Have sprung to the surface from nothing.
I am sparks, and catalysts, and life.

And you're telling me I can't?

Think again.

NO.19 YOU

LISA MARIE SNEIJDER

Slow vibrations
Digital waves in past tense
A lifeline lost

Yesterdays
In spiky rhythms
Laughing at ungodly hours
Resonating sounds
No more wariness

Calling
Without a sudden morning rise
Leaving such abundance
Swallowed by absence

Letters in pixels
Filled with harmony
Becoming temporary glitches
Consumed in permanency

How can
Such wicked orderliness
Dismantle
The thin thread of memory

NO.20

I'M NO JELLYFISH

ZOE BOTT

I'M NO JELLY FISH

NO.21

JÖKULMÆR

ARÍEL BERTELSEN

In the unbreathable heat,
my body racked a sob,
a cry.
A cry for home,
for something to feel like heim,
heima.
And somehow my own hands
dug you up from the earth,
a piece of home.

Green eyes shining with the speckled colours
of norðurljós.
Skin like snjófall and birch bark,
freckles of olivine.
Lips like newly picked blueberries
about to burst under your teeth,
coloured in lingonberries,
krækiber stained tongue.
I lay upon your thighs,
in your groin of pillowy moss.

And the moles that dot your body,
your chocolate marks,
I left there with my kisses.
I trail your body,
up,
upp.

At the back of your neck;
a white mark,
from a time when you laid
with an elf.
The nights you danced with them,
when you forgot your name,
I whispered it back.

The names you gave me,
the ones you changed.
A rose did not fit me.
Rather I should be a forget-me-not,
gleym-mér-ei,
because you would never forget me.
Now you whisper the same.

Humming along to Bubba
came like a rumble in your chest,
another earthquake in the warmth
of the earth.
Smoke floats out of your cracks,
into the cold loft,
but it is not reykur at all
but vapour
in your misnamed
Valley of Smoke.
Your sweet vapour strokes my
thighs with a wet kiss,
a paintbrush,
a blooming of poppies and pansies.

Your eyes catch me,
fiðringur up my stomach,
as a looming stone figure
atop your breast
stands guard.
I look up, past your mounds

your curves and his gaze,
to gorgeous Fjalladrottning mín.

My Jökulmær,
come to me in dreams.
Held in your embrace,
blueberries against my nape,
and with whimpers
my Norðurey's fingertips
grace my pearl.
Sjáumst,
in an airport,
next time it will be mine.
Sjáumst,
in a snow pile,
while you pick snjókorn out of my gold.
Hittumst,
in the corner of a bar,
á morgun if you would like.
Hittumst,
wherever you'd like.

NO.22

MAN ON THE MOON

FELICIA BECK

Dear Neil Armstrong,

When I look up at the sky, I look at you.

All those twinkling stars, your twinkling smile, and I look and look and look, and the floor beneath me is so soft and you're under the dirt, you're under the grass, you're under this stone, down beneath the layers, down, down, down, but up in the night sky and everywhere all at once.

They said you were crazy, yes they did; they laughed and shook their heads at your determination, and they didn't believe anything you said, and don't you think they would have locked you up if they could? Crushing iron bars, shrinking prison cell, wood on all sides, and the earth wants to join you in the coffin, find you under the grass somewhere, hiding just out of sight.

The moon! That's what I meant to say, the moon, moon, moon, moon, moon, because you were there, that's what they found out, you made it up there, you did it. Stepping on the moon, touching the moon, picking the moon up in your hands and storing it in your heart and you're a hero! No ridicule anymore, no, no, no. You, up in the sky and them, stuck down here.

Chilly night, chilly wind, silver moon, you're up there. Saving a country that didn't need saving, or maybe it did, you did it, hero! They won't let me see you, I asked and asked and asked, and I know you're not busy, I know you're rotting away under the ground, but they're not letting me visit and I need to, need to see you, need to know you're real, I need to talk to you, hero.

Stars shine through metal bars, but it's so beautiful, the moonlight, so soft.

Reach out and touch it. Burns!

Moon so far away, stars so far away, what's it like going to a place no one's ever gone? There's no air on the moon, no air to breathe, how'd you breathe on the moon! What's it like breathing on the moon! Gasp in, gasp out, look, I'm breathing in the moonlight! Just like you, hero, hero!

Everyone knows your name; you've been on the tv, you've been on the moon, the moon, the moon, the moon way high up in the sky beyond the earth, beyond life, beyond anything here. What's really here and why are we here and why am I not up on the moon with you? I want to feel the moon, I want to touch the moon, like you hero, hero! To do something no one's done!

But they won't let me visit you, they won't let me out, they won't let me out, THEY WON'T LET ME OUT!

I'll see you under the dirt, Mr. Armstrong. I'll be meeting you there soon. If that's the only way to thank you. That's where I'll be. Under the dirt. To talk to you. Soon. And then we'll be laughing up among the stars.

Not rotting away in a cell.

[*Unsent letter discovered in Southern Ohio Correctional Facility, discarded on the floor beneath the dangling legs of Inmate C88193*]

NO.23

WITHERED CHATEAU

ANASTAZIA WALSH-STRANGE

All stories begin with a place, so I shall take you home. It lies beyond the weeping willow trees, barren of love and leaves, and just across the world. I saw the faces of those drooping branches, whistling in the autumnal wind. Your face matched the little world we walked into – mute. Each tree greeted us like homely guardians of the forgotten age and howled with the voice of dead men.

This place creaks with leery bones and I laugh. Because although I now live alone, I am with ancestors sown into the ground. You witnessed it in full. I swung open the grand doors that were inlaid with the symbols of my once prestigious house. Lost and forgotten was each tightly-strung wooden knot that ran down the door.

But I brought up that burnt-up childhood. The old walls of these hallowed halls smell like butterflies and filth. I had pinned them to the living room. I stuck them down and pricked them with little pins. With force.

These creatures make a great display; for each of them have a dark and hypnotic pattern. If you stare too long, you forget this befouled house. The *Vanessa cardui* hangs up there, fully preserved. It is pale with buffy-orange and black tips, marked with white spots. It's disgustingly common; and they dare to call it the painted lady.

I stuck it here, with purpose. I want to see you squirm.

Observe its beauty because I know you hate it.

NO.24
MUGDOCK CASTLE

MARISA SPENCE

NO.25

NOMADIC TENTACLES FOR NATURE

STAN DIMITROV

the smell of faeces signalled rain
the fog enfolded tall tectonic plates
my morning coffee view a poets inspiration

it allied familiarity of the setting a societal neglect where no
two eyes were raw and no voice was unheeded where bikes
were fast enough to reach the commencement and end and
save the world from sixes and eights

when i gazed i was tranquilled
predictable scenic imprinted in my mind
i seeked a touch of the unknown
fleeing from the alps to the thames
from an oval of nature to a circle of despondency
rather the steel and glassy castles
than peaceable sound of freedom

the small was too small i longed for the pace
i longed for opportunities and a smile on my face
i entered a battlefield aconitine a war
see the shine of my dreams diminish with every word
submitted

weekends would come and the office shut
local parks welcomed best chances of regaining
people laughing children running
dogs chasing birds fishes jumping
sinsemilla dominating breaths and hippie music
all lives colourful for a good forty-eight hours
i sat there wondering when i would be taken back
to my known green to nature
that nurtured my soul

every face i met yearned to be back home
and home was always floral and characteristic with
personality

NO.26

PREPARED FOR BATTLE

LIBERTY RAINBIRD - JERVIS

went in armed, prepared for battle

But all I found was

Still

Quiet

Calm

And so I left...

Leaving my troubles behind me.

NO.27

REDWOODS

MARISA SPENCE

NO.28

SMOKE AND COLOURS

FELICIA BECK

There is darkness.

He opens his eyes.

To his right is a thick, suffocating cloud of smoke, but to his left are colours.

Wow! Such beautiful colours.

Glittering drips of orange, wide stretches of deep blue, spots of green shining here and there, all around.

Look at them dancing in the cool breeze! Look at them twisting and twirling and laughing and smiling!

Now he's laughing too, stepping deep within the colours, watching as they whirl around and envelop his body.

The air here is light and fresh, and he reaches out to join them, to disperse into a lovely mist and float away, to become the brightness.

Hello, blue! Hello, purple! Hello...

Red?

No!

The colours are gone. Dispersed. Despaired.

He's shaking and his heart is hammering and all that's left is a blankness, an emptiness, a memory he doesn't want to remember and a colour he can't forget.

He blinks and blinks. His vision is hazy and he can't make

out any of the shapes in front of him, and he doesn't know if he wants to.

He doesn't want to see the colours anymore. He doesn't want to think of them.

The thick, suffocating cloud is still at his right. This time, when he looks at it, there is nothing to whirl around and protect him.

He is crushed.

Dense, acrid smoke funnels into his lungs, stinging his nose and eyes. The air is oppressive and heavy, smelling of burning and pain and mistakes.

He cries out, but he can't hear himself.

The grey smoke condenses further, tightening its pressure on his body. There's nothing he can do to stop this, nowhere he can escape, it's dark and chaotic and ashy. His vision goes black and all he can think of is red, red, red, red.

Red fire scorching a red coat. Red blood glistening on red skin. Red lips gurgling red spit. Red heart beating to a red stop.

Stop!

There's no smoke.

Trembling lungs shakily accept clean air. Stiff hands unclench. Stinging eyes open.

He's lying in bed.

It's a soft bed, dipping under his weight and cocooning him gently. The blanket is draped neatly over his body, its silky smoothness cool against his hot skin.

His limbs ache and refuse to move. He is a stone statue.

His eyes blink up at the ceiling.

The room is lit up in a hazy glow, rays of sunlight slipping between the cracks of the blinds. Daytime.

He stays motionless.

The fog might not be smothering the room, but it is still there. Inside him.

He must have inhaled it.

It sits like a heavy weight on his brain, pressing dully and thudding with his heartbeat, coating his mind in a dense haze.

He can't remember what he did yesterday. He can't

remember what he's supposed to be doing today. He doesn't even know what day it is.

It's something of a relief.

He lets his eyes close. There is a beat of peace, until rationality takes hold.

In the darkness of his mind, with nothing to distract him, he can feel the thick fog ebbing away, wisps slipping out of his ears. The answers are sitting there, waiting to be remembered, demanding to be heard.

His tired eyes snap open.

The smoke rushes back, smothering clarity, and he slips into the safety of oblivion.

He does not shut his eyes again.

The ceiling has fourteen cracks running across its surface. One is bigger than the others. It creaks and gapes and strains. He wonders how the roof has not caved in yet, wonders when it will finally give in.

He imagines the wood crashing down into the room, snapping his bones and burying him in a pile of secrets.

The crack widens.

He watches.

He blinks and his eyes burn and he blinks again and now the room is dark.

The ceiling is lost to a shadow of gloom. The cracks are no longer visible.

Night has come.

He slowly turns on his side and reaches out a trembling arm.

The pillow beside his is empty.

What is going on? This is not right. It should not be like that. Where is she?

The smoke tunnels down to his heart and he chokes. He does not want to look at the forlorn pillow on the forgotten side of the bed.

He thinks of knocking it to the floor, but his arm is too heavy. Instead, he heaves himself up, unable to stay in this bed any longer.

Halting steps propel him outside; a spirit drifting around,

unseen in the shadowy dark.

The moon is high in the sky, glittering ominously in its place among the stars.

It winks at him, and he averts his gaze.

The pavement is rough and chilly under his bare feet, and it scrapes and tears at his flesh as he takes a step, and another, and another...

The next step is soft, and he registers dirt and damp leaves stroking his skin, embracing his presence.

Trees begin to crowd him, stepping out of the darkness to say hello, and he examines them. Their branches rustle in the wind, waving. He decides he would like to get lost among the trees.

He spins around, clapping his hands together, watching with wide eyes as the trees form a ring, more and more arriving to shield him from the outside world. All he can hear is the whisper of their leaves and his own panting breath, penetrating the silence of the night.

It's a forest he's in now, a proper forest, and he decides it's safe to sit in the dirt against a tree trunk and let his body go limp.

The last of the thick fog in his brain is expelled into the cool air as he sighs, but he has nothing to fear from his thoughts here in this forest. He lets it go, watching it escape up into the sky.

His mind is clear at last.

It's not the oppressive, choking clarity that he fears. No, this is pleasant and free. His thoughts flow in a stream of contentment, bringing his attention to the surrounding outdoors, the nature forming a protective bubble over his being.

Here, he is a safe, solitary figure, tucked away from the world, calmly existing.

There is a curious rustling from somewhere to his right, slowly increasing in volume. He turns his head, back still comfortably resting against the tree trunk, curious but not worried.

From behind the dense mass of foliage steps a jaguar.

It wears the night like a coat, slinking and blending into the dark with its obsidian fur, but its amber eyes gleam brightly in contrast, staring into his widening blue ones.

He watches, motionless, as it creeps forward, closer and closer.

It comes to a halt in front of him.

'Hello, stranger,' the jaguar croaks, sitting on its hind legs. Its voice is hoarse from disuse. It must not often have had cause to speak.

He tries to smile, but his mouth doesn't obey. 'Hello,' he says finally, blankly.

The jaguar's tail twitches. 'You look like you're a long way from home.' The words are void of judgement.

There's a pause.

'I have no home,' he tells the animal.

'Is that so?' the jaguar asks, cocking its head.

A bird chirps from somewhere high above. He lets his gaze drift upward.

The sky is brightening, streaks of yellow chasing away the dark and arcing across an ocean of blue. In the light, the jaguar's black coat gleams, framed against the dullness of the tree trunks.

'Why do you have no home?' the jaguar questions, voice strengthening to a silky purr. 'What happened?'

He doesn't like those questions. They're too real.

Memories of his home and his life and her start to flash and dart through his mind, but underneath it all he can sense the blistering, choking grip of red, red, red. He's not ready to remember, not yet, he can't possibly remember, but he doesn't know where to hide—

'In my forest, we like to forget, too,' the jaguar croons. It offers a paw.

He stands and takes it, the velvety fur and rough pads warm under his trembling fingers. The jaguar leads him deeper among the trees, away from the sunlight and the birds and the memories.

It suddenly turns to face him, breath hot on his skin, and leans forward. Sharp teeth clamp down on his neck, slicing through his skin, but there's no pain, just a rush of dizziness, and then the jaguar draws away.

The world around him begins to twist and morph and blur and oh!

The colours are back! Spinning and swirling joyfully, welcoming him in.

'Let us dance,' the jaguar's voice echoes. He can no longer see the creature, can no longer feel its grip, but he knows it doesn't matter.

His spirits are lifted. Look at the lights floating around him!

Splashes of blue wink in and out, diamonds of orange dart and pulsate, ribbons of green spiral in a shimmer of light.

It's numbing and hypnotic and he is one with his surroundings.

His body sways, limbs flopping aimlessly, but his eyes are bright with interest, drinking in the vibrance.

The jaguar is still here. He can't see it, but he feels its presence, shining through the dashes of purple, smiling among the glimmers of yellow.

He opens his mouth to speak to it, but the motion sends a jolt through his body, jarring him to his core. The colours flee in fear of the room materialising around him.

He's lying in bed.

The room is filled with bright light. The space beside him is empty.

His chest tightens.

He doesn't like the way the truth is trying to burst forth from its cage. He can feel memories attacking the wall constraining them, violently clawing at the hastily constructed layers. His mind is imploding on itself.

He wishes he could bring back the colours, but like before, they're long gone.

'Hello, jaguar,' he says instead. 'Hello, hello.' Jaguar, jungle, jungle, jaguar. The safety of trees under the cover of night. Come back, please come back.

But the jaguar doesn't respond, and he doesn't have the energy to walk back to the forest. It's all over because the block in his mind crumbles to piles of rubble and grief. There's ash coating the floor and screams on her lips and red blood smeared over his hands, and he's choking on smoke and his own sobs, clutching at her charred flesh, begging her to stay with him, please, please, and he knows it's too late, please...

He's struggling out of bed, gasping and heaving, the room warping around him, stumbles to the bathroom and collapses heavily in front of the toilet to vomit out the guilt sloshing in his stomach.

It's too much, it's too much, it's his fault and he can't run anymore. The truth is shattered in pieces around him, cutting him open and charring his insides.

The forest wasn't real, the colours were never there. He's just a broken man kneeling on his bathroom floor because he can't handle her death.

Wiping his mouth with a sloppy swipe of a hand, he has just enough strength to crawl to the counter, thrust himself upright, and stare at his wretched reflection in the mirror.

He's looking at a soul removed from reality, a pathetic creature desperate for a comfort he doesn't deserve, a liar, liar, liar!

A sharp pain suddenly catches his attention, and his eyes trail down, coming to an abrupt stop to stare at fresh blood (it's his, not hers, not hers, not hers) dripping down his neck.

His fingers come up to press against the wound, heedless of the stinging, exploring the two gaping holes.

There's no mistaking it.

A jaguar bite.

NO.29

TEMPTATION STAIRWAY

ANASTAZIA WALSH-STRANGE

A singular staircase
White imbued
That runs up and up and up
Straight to you
I step
No other path
To light my journey

When I climb
Above is the sky
No line
It's fine
I will take the risk

A singular staircase
When I climb
Pink smoke
Blue mist
A blank cosmos
Little lights
Little stars
Morphing shapes
All forever far

When I climb
I feel the hope
I do not feel
The everlasting slope
Round and round
No rails for balance
Constant humming
Absent ballad

A singular staircase
Endless down
Forever far
Is the journey down
Little lights
Pink smoke
When I fall
I wish that Hope
Will catch me
Otherwise
White void will damn me

No. 30

The Ignored Symptom of the Pandemic

BEX EASTWELL

My safe place turned into a prison. Caged inside,
I withered away sat in front of screens.
First YouTube, Zoom and Teams, then Netflix. I'd
much rather sleep the day away. Vaccines
were being shipped out. But I'm at the end
of the list, not a priority. Can't face
it, getting out of bed, the house. Don't tend
to move. Body atrophying in place.

Then, we are set free. Shops open, clubs turn
to bars and life resumes. The classes are
in lecture halls. The students return.
My friends come over for drinks. It's bizarre.

I am still stuck. My muscles are frozen, my heart
will start to pound. Won't leave. I've come apart.

NO. 31
TROLL TOLL

BLU SELBY

NO.32

THE CHARM OF CAPITALISM

FELICIA BECK

Don't speak as you're sorted, silent subjugation
Creeping up forward, food cans for each one
Caution now, steady now, scramble away
Careful surviving another cruel day

This is the life of the dregs of the land
Ground in the grip of the invisible hand
Slipping in slime and the waste of the earth
Inheriting debits, unsure of your worth

Recycled items, now nothing is new
But the head is the head and the shoe is the shoe
Don't question your place, no analysis
Freeloaders are lower and that's how it is

This is the way mankind's meant to be
If you were destined for wealth, you'd already be free
But look at you now, all the sweat and the grime
Shaky and cagey, a corpse in no time

Without inequity there could be no peace
If wealth trickled down it would only decrease
Once you work and you break and your motivation is gone
You'll be crushed into grease as the system chugs on

There must be a meaning to life, that is true
So why would you deny it might be servitude?
It sets a bad example, this sudden outcry
We'll deny it later, but you're going to die.

NO.33

THE EDGE OF THE GALAXY

MARISA SPENCE

NO.34

هوئے ہوئے شہزادی: THE LOST PRINCESS

ISHA JAN

NO.35
THE OLD HOUSE

GABRIEL LIU

My toy box was a never-changing cottage with a long corridor.

CREAK

THE OLD HOUSE

Grandpa thought the security door was too squeaky.

And no one bothered to fix the wall.

On the right inside, there would be an emergency shelf, but there was never an emergency.

I always wondered, if a fugitive was hiding there, leaving traces of life.

On the right, I would greet Grandma's sewing machine and Grandpa's parents.

"GOOD MORNING!"

"...good morning..."

She would always say, "If you stay here any longer, you would start growing MOULD!"

And I would say "But—

there is sooo much fun here!"

I would drift into day-dream in the smell of washed duvet.

But there was no duvet, only dust.

So I thought,

It must be the scent of sparkling dust.

If I got bored, I would open that out-of-tune piano,

and pretend to be a composer in misery.

Or I would drag my dolls there, and turn the sofa into a trampoline.

I always believe the higher I bounced, the livelier they could be.

But there were times I had to settle down...

CREAK

There was no ticking clock, but the rhythm of the sewing machine,

But still......

I know everything has to change.

NO. 36

THE OLD MAN AND THE TEA

MARIA NAE

It was a cloudy Sunday afternoon when the old man walked through the door. He sat in his usual chair facing the window that looked upon the busy street. People walked rapidly past each other and past their youths, chasing ephemeral happiness that would leave them wanting more. The old man smiled one of those smiles that comes with wisdom beyond the evident years that marked his face and soul. A smile that you only see four or five times in a lifespan. He was like that too, once.

'Good afternoon. What will it be today?' A young waitress asked, tapping her pen against her notepad with an unnecessary urgency.

'A cup of Earl Grey, please,' the man replied, his voice resonating through the empty café.

He was an ordinary man, with ordinary features. His fisherman's hat was tilted to one side, revealing a patch of fine, white hair cascading against his sunburnt skin. He wore a beige shirt and brown trousers tucked into his black boots. Wrinkles ran down his face like rivers converging at the edges of his eyes. His hazel eyes were deep, as if they had been brewing the secrets of the world over his eighty-two years.

'Here you go,' the waitress whispered as she placed the cup on the table. She brought milk and sugar.

The man cradled the hot cup between his coarse palms for a moment before allowing his cracked lips to touch the smooth liquid. He took a sip and closed his eyes. The rich flavour slid down his throat and hugged his soul in a warm embrace.

'Mmm,' he murmured.

It was a sunny Sunday morning. A man and his son were walking on the docks towards a small fishing boat. They embarked and rowed until a sea of blue glitter, stretching out before them, was all they could see. Silence surrounded them and with it came a sense of absolute peace. The warm breeze against their skin, the smell of salty water and the occasional seagull flying above made them feel free. This was their moment and they would cherish its sanctity forever.

'You wake up at 4am and stay out all day, then end up in that café spending all our money! Is that what you want to teach our son?' the mother would scold. 'You never catch anything anyway.'

The man and his son locked their gazes. The corners of their mouths slowly turned upwards and the father signalled the boy to be quiet. She would never understand.

The old man placed the empty cup on the table and staggered to his feet. He lowered his head towards the waitresses and made his way to the door.

'Does he come here often?' One waitress whispered.

'Every Sunday,' the other replied. 'They say his father was a fisherman.'

NO.37

THE RED LIGHT DISTRICT

JASMINE HIGGINS

i suppose if it's going to happen anyway
it's best that we can see they're safe
we can keep an eye on the hunters
and their intentions with people's bodies;
people's homes

but foreign to my culture,
i feel unsettled by the normality:
people coming and going
children walking home from school
past women in boxes and little clothing
tourists gawking, picking their favourite
to get the full experience of this city

i am torn, aching for the women
many of whom may be happy
but all of them, certainly not
glowing pretty in red
mesmerizing lights against soft skin
angelic bodies, undeniably priceless

if i was in a room like that,
i'd swallow the key and turn off all the lights
maybe that's just me
maybe i'm afraid of men
but who isn't?

i don't know if this place is beautiful or terrifying.
all i know is when the girl behind the glass smiles at me,
i smile back.

NO.38

THE REMNANTS OF AMHOLLOW HOUSE

MORGAN BRATLI

I wormed through the thick stew of souls. Keen needles deafened the awareness of my insight, somehow innate in their ability to unearth the spots most tender. Puncturing once, twice, sewing over-under arteries, pulling, and tightening. The phantom blood ran warmly beneath the cranium, red slugs rolling from under the eyelid, staining the optic globe with pink varnish. No cure for this curse dwelled in the pocket. But be poised! And wait perhaps for bile, for a half-digested meal, wanting escape from its damp cavern, to stir and relieve the misery. I yearned to conceive miraculous abilities, then the words leaking from me would form forbidden spells and frighten the needles abroad forevermore. Whatever judgement might burden me for such witchcraft, I would meet with unending defiance.

Alas, the illusory hexes never took root, and for long the throes haunted my mettle. For long I cooled my heels, beseeching it to pass. Yet, quickly as they had invaded me, the anguish and qualms vanished away. I awoke from the nightmare, smelling gusts of fruit and bread from the brown bag in my embrace. Burning within me, the singular ambition to arrive home and submit to a long sugary dream.

The blue spill of moonlight glowed on dewed buildings, appearing almost to melt their uneven brickwork.

I wanted away from the suffocating town. Away from the sooty fogs that soiled the London air, the stench of river Thames and the vexing clip-clop of horses on cobblestones. Londoners shuffled about, not one of them talking; mere hovering faces of bluish pallor, offering neither helloes nor goodbyes. They oppressed me, insulted me, cutting into my body with their wide perforating looks. I wanted away.

The beast played an upend tune, inspiring murder by closing of June.

Where on earth had these absurd words come from? I had never before heard them, thought them, or allowed my larynx to produce them. Now they are repeated as the looping strains of a wind-up music box. It was some fragment of a droll nursery rhyme – yes, a fair story. Or was it him over there, thin-lipped and smiling in the darkened archway, who had breathed the strange phrase? What had him watching my apples and bread in such vile scrutiny? Was he a greedy vagabond, wanting a generous donation for his supper? No, I judged him to be far too spruce and unspotted in coat and trousers. It would take some nerve to beg for coin, wearing flawless wools. Rain or shine, not a single crumb would I share.

'Apples and bread. The dread, the dread! Fancy feast to keep yourself fed?' said the man and displayed teeth, shaking with mirth. It sickened me to the core, and how sickening indeed to approach me on the sore subject. He had seen the volunteers hand me my supper to be sure, thinking then of his noxious poem. Did he believe I required an expensive steak to satisfy my belly, that I sought some arbitrary lavishness in my meals? Beyond the shadow of a doubt could I afford the finest piece of succulent meat on display, but simply chose to make use of the opportunities that were. Curdling cur, I'd have him choking on his sable-silk cravat.

He flickered in surprise. His eye uncloaked and opaque, studying. Had he seen the insult float in my pupils? Had the ball of light in my eye flickered in morse? I retreated, averting my step to avoid the string of shadow between the lamps in the street. A repressive sight stretched above them, in the sky, of a lone moon bullied by serpentine clouds. I sneaked a glance over my shoulder. The man walked, unblinking, a small yet thick book under his arm, stroking it with a red-gemmed thumb.

He made no effort to mask himself or dampen the clicking of his heels. I weaved myself through alleys, ducked under laundry, passed empty corners. I exploited the detours no lavish man would consider. But in each instance of looking behind, his stern strides and swelling coat were ever there. An inkblot against the sewer's smoke-breathing nostrils, pages fluttering as crows' wings along with a whirring chant I couldn't position.

Neglected flowerbeds lined windows where within white drapes stirred. Hogs Lane was deserted but for me and my shadow. For the briefest and perhaps foolish moment, I thought myself alone. The shadow belonged not to me, but a creature whose light steps fell out of tandem with my own.

Flutter.

At this sound, my fingers probed nook and depth inside my pocket until touching rough metal. The brass saviour merged with my hand as I saw home. That derelict manor named Amhollow, waiting by the treeline's gnarled toes. That spot of landscape where heathers glowed with a purple hue, a feeble gleam of hope. 'I have your key,' said I, cloaking the words in whispers and unable to stop the phrase spilling out again and again. I turned the key – opened, closed the door – and turned it once more.

Door locked. Man away. Yes, surely. Away...

Faster than a rat scurrying from a broom, I retreated to the only room I cared to occupy. Up the stairs, right of the front door, and then right again. This path I knew and need know nothing more. T   he journey of creaking wood that fathered my little cocoon. The swelling dark could stretch its fingers far and never gain on my swiftness.

In truth, they did frighten me, those murky spots fringing

.

the halls, the long faces on decomposing portraits, gleaming the same bluishness as London's people. My room, however – my sunny island in the black sea – I had made comfortable and pleasant enough. Towers of dust-powdered books obscured each but the north-east corner, where the bed awaited me with sheets askew. The fireplace, agape with no heat in its sooty gullet, held above its mantelpiece a lone painting, and for no lack of bravery had I turned this about with no recollection of its appearance whatsoever.

A cool dagger traced my spine. I deposited the brown bag of apple and bread beside my nightstand, sat down by the old davenport in my chair, and began recording the strange event in my journal. I did not know for how long I wrote but was thrown out of concentration by the light spray of night rain. Had I unlocked the window?

My eyes went back to the journal. I experienced utmost discomfort trying to read the words as I waited for the purply ink to retreat into the parchment. No words. None. The sharp contours of each vowel and consonant had been so rational, so fiery and mint. Now they insulted me with their anonymity, appearing as no more than a madman's scribbles or murky rivers, disobeying the rules of gravity. How funny. Ha-ha! A few needles remained after all. In a begrimed recess where surplus thoughts lay dead, little trumpet daffodils never to be watered.

The bed, far to the north-east, summoned me, singing me a sweet lullaby. And I tried to sleep, oh how I tried! So intensely did I want to ingest that thin soup of rest, though the drops frightened little tadpoles. Then, either born from delirium or downright mania, I grew intensely paranoid. I could feel a thing by my window and though high above the heathers – shapes floated there, shadows bloomed. A snake curled up. Rats pitter-pattered in the walls. It was them, the wind and naught else.

The red slug squirmed. No one ever came here. No one in but a sorry state would come waltzing down this curling street which had only an end...

House sparrows blossomed into song as I awoke. Gone had the night, leaking into the room a warm glow of buttered light! Born within me grew such a profound relief, a glorious relief, in seeing morning penetrate the drapes. I offered my thanks to the heavens, to the morning dew, the grass and the house sparrows – everything! Never had I known or flirted with piousness, but in those wonderful moments I experienced a most holy delight, a sort of warmth deep in my lungs, at the flowery scent of nature's breeze pouring in the window. God was most deserving of prayer for bestowing this morning unto the world and for bringing my spirits aloft. I sprang from under the sheets and kneeled, elbows on mattress, fingers interwoven. The prayer was shrill, but I hoped with optimism that God had no qualms with my spasmodic lungs and would hear me natheless.

I lingered by the bed's edge for a long while, basking in newfound solemn devotion. Half in sleep, and pondering over my fresh sanity, my mouth began to water for the food I had no want for in yesterday's state. I had behaved a fool, allowed a stranger to unhinge me while the cure to my frenzy was simply a night of sleep, but for the life of me did I struggle to recall when I had succumbed to it. There was something... from the final seconds of yesterday's memory – a sound. An unbroken melodic wailing, from somewhere beyond my door. A draught, echoing down the halls? May be, may be. It mattered little. The world, after all, spun once again on a steady axis.

But disaster struck. My apple! Shrunk to seeds alongside crumbs of bread! What was it, had I devoured my supper without memory of it? No, of course not. My hungered belly argued otherwise. Deep down, I knew. Fat, gluttonous rats had come to feast while I slept!

I kneeled dog-like, thirsting for rodent blood. 'Come out,' yelled I. 'Fiends!' Scarpering, laughing, I heard them. Giving me insult, squeaking all manner of gossip and filthy lies.

Ha! Shameful! How had my thoughts and marrow grown so grossly blackened by so little a thing? My eye searched for any modicum of solace, then found an open journal. There in the abyss of ink – by God! Where I had traced an incomprehensible mess in some vacant state of mind, a wide-eyed pig stared back. Towering over it, a nebulous figure. Inhuman. Of no structure.

From the manor's sequestered bowels, wailing echoed afresh. Louder, louder still. Probing, splitting, pupils aflame. 'Begone!' It would not go. He would not. He watched. Full of pungent hatred, he judged the world with perverted mirth. Cravat of sable silk and a gemmed thumb. Above the sooty mouth, a portrait so alive!

Books fell. I flung shut the door behind me, sinking to the floor. The cavernous gullet of the corridor stretched endlessly. Faces in golden rims leered, uttering unified nasal hums.

A tiny flicker of light danced beside me, drowning in a pool of wax. Yet I clung to it, vowing to keep it afloat.

I raised the candle high, walked down crumbling stairs and past doors in the swirling, wizened palm of blackness. Cruel eyes in painted faces wandered over me, mouths aloud in thrums, beckoning me on. 'Unveil us,' they sang. The wailing grew. All that remained – a door. Creaking open, leaking sweet-foul odours. Within, a mere shape and the glint of two unblinking spheres hovered. Atop a barrel, he sat violating the strings of an upend fiddle. He breathed a damp wind, needling my pores. The light died. In that final flicker, I bore witness to its unspeakable wholeness.

'Come, little pig-man. Squeal. Scream. With mine music, I will make you as mad as you seem.' Words—things! From my convulsing throat. Vibrating optic globes. Red slugs gushing.

This place...

Heathers of reddish-blue, as alluring amethysts; yet empty, abandoned, and hollow where naught else grows. A home for rats and snakes. Perhaps one day it would thrive and bloom further to bring the heathers company. The dying wisps of spring would beckon the trees to fruit and spawn bushes ripe to berry. By next June on this same day, without me, life would be plenty.

I squealed and screamed.

NO.39

THE SOUND OF
YOUR CASSETTES

STAN DIMITROV

black and white and yellow were your cassettes
the ones you used to play alone or with me
on a gathering at the sea
the rock pop jazz and blues
none of them i liked but the view of happy you

plastic shaped a rectangular container
with the holes and moulds and spools
throwing magnetic tapes across each other
it sounds like a simple thing but this was
miraculous to me

how could one such a small object
bring you such a smile ear to ear
though when i asked you something or wanted to hear
your smile dimmed like how the bugs hid
the cold basements lights

how you picked each tape carefully knowing
each holds its own story
a different song played by different people
how you knew exactly which one you needed
for your different moods

but i wish you listened to the cassette
labelled with my name

that little piece of plastic
hidden in the bottom of the black shoe box
with dulled corners to a wrinkled lid
paint worn out by hands always grabbing the same corner
to lift it up but never dig down

i saw you looking at it once
the black sheep that imprisons my vocals
though its tape is brand new
its shape holds no more fingerprints
its spools never made a circle

now im coming back to this old lifeless house to see
what it was back then just brother you and me
but i end up holding your cassettes
my enemies the ones that made you forget
you had a son with a voice
so gentle and loving

traumatising as it is
im still muted

TIME

LISA MARIE SNEIJDER

When devoured by loneliness
Where no bird chirps for morning glory
Waiting to be
Oh so patiently

Still gathering the time till it creeps hour by hour
And sundown and sunrise are bleak
Nonetheless shimmer

With flickering melodies alluring a daily spell
It's a relative concept of being
But it floats and hovers
On to stillness

Let it rest
Till sundown where the unknown thrives
And preconceived conceptions vanish
Hiding in dusky gushes of promise

Impatience is sinning
With pleasure that is
Still pressing the inconsolable feeling of nothingness

NO.41
THE TICK OF MEMORY
WEI XINWEI

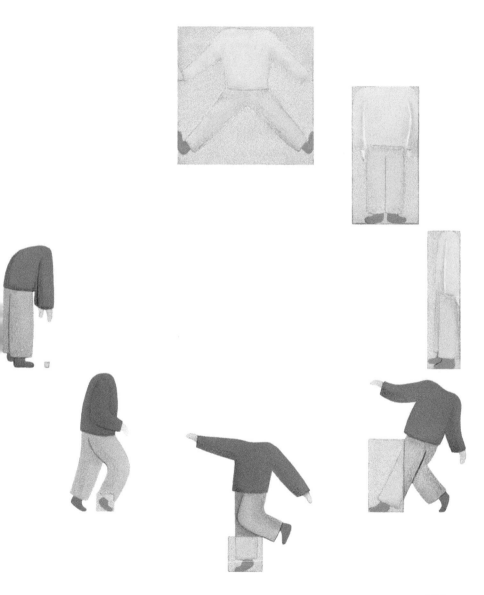

2022
THIS YEAR'S CREATIVES

RAAJEEV AUCHAMBIT
Raajeev Auchambit writes poetry and prose fiction. His previous short story, '1968–2020: (De) Fame of Liberation' was shortlisted by the Ministry of Arts and Culture for its retrospective on the pains and pleasures of the Republic of Mauritius.

FELICIA BECK
Felicia Beck majors in History and Literature. In both fields, she aims to explore the power of written works and the unspoken intentions of their authors. While working towards her goal of qualifying as a teacher, she hopes to publish further pieces along the way.

ARÍEL BERTELSEN
Aríel Bertelsen is an aspiring author with an Icelandic and Spanish background. She writes poetry and prose about queer and Nordic themes, as well as philosophical, surrealist, and fantasy genres.

ZOE BOTT
Zoe Bott's background in journalism has shown her the importance of raising awareness about climate change. Her piece, I'm No Jellyfish, is a response to the shocking fact that over half of the world's turtles have eaten plastic because they cannot differentiate plastic bags from their main foodsource, jellyfish.

MORGAN BRATLI

Morgan Bratli is a third-year student of BA Creative Writing and Film Cultures. He enjoys exploring darker themes in his work and has previously been featured in the 2020 and 2021 editions of RiPPLE.

CLARA CHACON GAMARRA

Clara Chacon Gamarra is a BA Illustration student from Bolivia. She writes for self-reflection and self-entertainment. Her work here is a revisited edition of poetry dating from 2014-2016.

STAN DIMITROV

Stan Dimitrov is a Creative and Professional Writing student whose poetry has also been featured in the 2021 edition of RiPPLE.

BEX EASTWELL

Bex Eastwell is an MA Creative Writing and Publishing student. Her ultimate ambition is to become a published novelist and poet. She is currently working on a first draft of a full-length crime novel and a collection of poetry.

RACHEL ESSEX

Rachel Essex is a Creative Writing student from Yorkshire. With a passion for storytelling, she dreams of spending her days reading, writing, and performin (while eating Yorkshire puddings!).

JASMINE HIGGINS

Jasmine Higgins is a self-published poet. Her book, *A Girl Is A Shapeshifter*, was released in 2019; and in 2020 it was featured in the anthology, *Sunday Mornings At The River*. She is currently working on her next poetry collection which she hopes to publish this year.

ISHA JAN

Isha Jan's photograph was taken to highlight the absence of South Asian representation in Disney films. She hopes to spread awareness around this issue with her work.

DANIELLE KNIGHT

Danielle Knight is an MA Creative Writing & Publishing student whose work explores fantasy and fairytale themes.

GABRIEL LIU

Gabriel Liu is an international student from Hong Kong, currently working towards her BA in Illustration. She aims to combine imagery with stories that are often forgotten by others, and hopes to gain experience at zine fairs in the future.

CAMERON MOWAT

Cameron Mowat's work was undertaken across sites in Hampton Wick Gardens, Hampton Court Park, and Thames Ditton. He is inspired by earth soil material research, and created the piece as a form of a communication to his future self.

MARIA NAE

Maria Nae is an MA Publishing student with a deep love of reading. Her favourite genres are fantasy and literary fiction, which inspire her to write short stories or reviews on her blog. She hopes to become an editor and one day help to bring beautiful stories to life.

SKYE PRICE

Skye Price is pursuing an MA in Creative Writing while working full-time as a teacher of secondary education. Her goal is to one day publish her own collection of poetry based around empowerment and healing.

LIBERTY RAINBIRD-JERVIS

Liberty Rainbird-Jervis is a Chemistry student at Kingston, who pursues her love of art and creative writing in her spare time.

BLU SELBY

Blu Selby's work often involves gems, taking any object she can find and adorning it with crystals. She aims to explore the line between contemporary art and design, and has been featured in magazines such as Dazed and The Perfect Magazine.

LISA MARIE SNEIJDER

Lisa Marie Sneijder is a Curating Contemporary Design MA student. She has written an award-winning thesis on the decolonial aesthetics of the Black Panther Party and currently works as an editor for Tijdschrift Kuntslicht.

MARISA SPENCE

Marisa Spence is a lifelong fan of photography. Originally from Seattle, she obtained a BA in Media Arts from St. Mary's University in Twickenham, then spent three years capturing magical memories as a photographer at Disneyland Resort in California. She utilises both film and digital mediums.

HANNAH TAYLOR

Hannah Taylor is an aspiring writer in the process of completing her first novel. She currently writes film articles online and aims to continue with film journalism after concluding her studies, pursuing short stories alongside this.

COURTNEY THOMPSON

Courtney Thompson is an international student from the United States pursuing an MA in Creative Writing and Publishing. She specialises in prose fiction across various genres and hopes to publish more of her work in the future.

MICHAEL VOWLES
Michael Vowles is an MA Publishing student, originally from Nailsea but currently based in London. In 2014, he graduated from the University of Winchester with a BA in Creative Writing and pursues his love of writing through blogging.

ANASTAZIA WALSH-STRANGE
Anastazia Walsh-Strange is a POC student currently studying Creative Writing, whose main interests are poetry and short stories.

WEI XINWEI
Wei Xinwei's work seeks to always capture untold perspectives to engage in complex topics, using illustration as a bridge between disciplines to facilitate new conversations. She is fascinated by human memory, emotion and relationships, which are major themes in the work featured here.

ABOUT KINGSTON UNIVERSITY PRESS

Kingston University Press has been publishing high-quality commercial and academic titles for nearly fifteen years. Our list has always reflected the diverse nature of the student and academic bodies at the university in ways that are designed to impact on debate, to hear new voices, to generate mutual understanding and to complement the values to which the university is committed.

Since 2017 all the books we have published have been produced by students on the MA Publishing and BA Publishing courses, bringing to life a range of community and creative projects. often partnering with organisations from our local community or poets from the university's vibrant writing community. While keeping true to our original mission, and maintaining our wide-ranging backlist titles, our most recent publishing focuses on bringing to the fore voices that reflect and appeal to our community at the university as well as the wider reading community of readers and writers in Kingston, the UK and beyond.

@KU_press

Lightning Source UK Ltd.
Milton Keynes UK
UKHW021311010522
402264UK00006B/294